Editor Fleur Robertson

Design Alyson Kyles

Photography © Dr Paul Larmour

Additional photography pp 9, 26, 40, 43

© Dr David Lawrence

Production Ruth Arthur, Karen Staff, Neil Randles

Director of Production Gerald Hughes

Published in Ireland by
Gill & Macmillan Ltd,
Goldenbridge, Dublin 8
with associated companies throughout the world

CLB 4990

Text © 1997 CLB International,
Godalming, Surrey

ISBN 0-7171-2691-9

Printed and bound in Singapore

Opposite: Patrick prevents hostile soldiers from
crossing the Ford of Hy Lilaig in pursuit of him.
According to this legend they all drowned.
Kilcurry (RC), Co. Louth

Saint Patrick
— in —
Stained Glass

Lesley Whiteside

Photography by Paul Larmour

GILL & MACMILLAN

INTRODUCTION

Patrick is Ireland's national saint. He holds this position not as the first person to bring the gospel to the country but because of the impact he made on Irish society. Traditionally it has been held that he was born about 390, began his mission to Ireland in 432 and died about 461. Many scholars now think that this time frame is about thirty years too early. As this argument shows, he is a rather shadowy figure. All that we know for certain is derived from his only two surviving writings, his *Confession* and his *Letter to the soldiers of Coroticus*. The *Confession* gives us quite a good idea of his spirituality but has few biographical details. Likewise, the *Letter* attacking the Scottish warlord who had slaughtered some of Patrick's new converts and taken others into slavery is scant on detail but fills out a picture of him as a dedicated missionary, stern, even fierce in the defence of his flock.

In the centuries after his death, so much legend developed about Patrick that it became difficult to separate the historical saint from the cult figure. In this book a clear distinction is made between the two: it is chiefly the historical Patrick who is presented but some of the best-known legends are included.

The Patrick of the stained glass window is largely the Patrick of legend. This is particularly true of windows made by the artists of An Túr Gloine, the Irish studio founded in 1903, and by Harry Clarke. Their work, like that of the newly founded national theatre, was a celebration of the Irish heritage, with its heroic tales and its distinctively Celtic ornamentation in manuscripts and metalwork. Not surprisingly, the most dramatic and colourful legends about Patrick were favourite themes.

An Túr Gloine was founded to improve the standard of Irish stained glass by the introduction of the principles of the Arts and Crafts movement. Nineteenth-century Irish glass was rarely inspirational but there is a great deal of very good English glass in Irish churches. The English artists whose work is included in this book gave a more straightforward picture of Patrick, emphasising his place as one of the great saints of the Western church and paying little attention to legend.

We should not, however, be dismissive of the legend, for history as we know it is a relatively modern discipline. In a largely illiterate society stories were generally passed on by word of mouth, allowing some elaboration before they were written down. The Patrician legends may not be factually true but they often tell us some truth about the saint.

Patrick gives his birthplace as 'Bannavem Taberniae', which may be Birdoswald, near Carlisle, in Cumbria. We cannot be sure of the location but we know that it was near the west coast of Britain, for he was at home when, aged sixteen, he was captured by a group of Irish raiders.

Patrick was born into an aristocratic family, which lived on an estate worked by slaves. His father, Calpurnius, was a local official of the Roman Empire, responsible for maintaining law and order and collecting taxes. Although imperial control was much weaker than it had previously been, Roman law and custom permeated British society. Latin was the language of the church and of the administration and Patrick would have been educated at home through Latin. Perhaps the abrupt end of his education explains why his command of the language is so poor.

Christianity was well established in Britain by then and Patrick was born into a Christian family. His father was a deacon and his grandfather, Potitus, a priest but Patrick admits that as a youth he 'did not know the true God' and paid no attention to church teaching. He regards his capture and captivity in Ireland as just punishment for his early behaviour.

Patrick was one of 'thousands of captives' taken to Ireland. There was a ready market for slaves, most of whom worked as agricultural labourers, and he spent his slavery as a shepherd.

Clayton & Bell, 1878, Christ Church Cathedral (C of I), Dublin

PATRIC

Salvation
is of
CHRIST
the
LORD

Patrick was lonely as he guarded his flock night and day, in all weathers, in the woods or on the mountains, but it may have been in the beauty of nature that he discovered God. During his time as a slave, he became aware of God's presence with him, his love of God grew stronger, and his devotion so deepened that he would happily say 'up to a hundred prayers in one day and almost as many in the night'.

After six years, Patrick had the first of the dreams in which he discovered God's plans for him. On hearing a voice saying: 'Look, your ship is ready,' he left the flock and made his way to a port, where he found a ship about to sail. What joy he must have felt as he saw the Irish coastline disappear from view!

Patrick probably hoped never to return but ironically, having first come bound as a common slave, he returned to Ireland some years later, 'bound by the Spirit … a slave of Christ', to preach the gospel. He says nothing about his training, ordination or appointment as a bishop in Ireland, but does relate another dream, in which the 'voice of the Irish' called him back to live among them. Although fifth-century Ireland was still largely pagan, there were scattered groups of Christians. Patrick was sent to minister to them.

Daniel Braniff, c.1975, St Donard's (C of I), Belfast

It is probable that Patrick came to the north-east of the country. Strangford Lough is celebrated as Patrick's landing-place on his return to Ireland and Saul as the place where he preached in a barn to Dichu, his first convert. Patrick does not name any of the places in which he worked, but the tradition linking him with Armagh predates the writings which sought to establish the primacy of Armagh on the basis that he was its founder. (Tirechán's *Memoirs* and *Sayings* of Patrick, Muirchú's *Life* and the *Book of the Angel* are included, along with Patrick's *Confession*, in the Book of Armagh, the earliest known copy of the New Testament to be made in Ireland.)

Muirchú tells a lovely story that Patrick asked a rich man called Daire for a hill-top site for a church. Daire at first refused but relented after his horse died and was restored to life by the saint. He and Patrick climbed the hill of Armagh, where they saw a hind and a fawn. Patrick lifted up the fawn, forbade anyone to kill it and then let it run free. The north altar of the church was supposedly positioned at the spot where Patrick found the fawn.

This window, depicting the laying of the foundation stone of the church in Armagh, implies a more elaborate structure than Patrick would have built but captures the excitement experienced as the young church grew.

Lavers & Barraud, c. 1865, St Patrick's Cathedral (C of I), Armagh

AD GLORIAM DEI ANNO DOMINI 445

Purser's gentle window emphasises Patrick's association with Armagh but reminds us that he probably extended his work south through Louth and Meath. It portrays Patrick standing in 'the flowery fields of Louth'. According to the legend, Patrick loved Louth and would have been happy to stay there but an angel came to him and told him to go north to found the See of Armagh. Patrick looked sadly at the beautiful meadow in front of him but set his face towards Armagh, saying, 'I give thanks to God.' In return for his obedience, the angel named the place 'the Beautiful Meadow' and promised that another British missionary would establish a church there.

Patrick mentions only one place in Ireland. Writing of his calling to return, he tells of a dream in which he heard 'the voice of those who lived near the wood of Voclut, which is close to the western sea'. With one voice they shouted: 'Holy boy, we ask you to come and walk among us again.' There is a good case for arguing from this mention that Voclut, convincingly identified as being in Mayo, was the place of Patrick's captivity. In any case, as the dream was instrumental in his eventual mission to Ireland, it is extremely likely that he travelled there, stopping at places along the way. This helps explain how almost every area has its own Patrician story.

Sarah Purser, 1909, Kilcurry (RC), Co. Louth

Patrick's writings show that, rather than concentrating on the Christian community, he devoted much of his time and energy to converting the pagan Irish. This may have been one of the reasons why he faced criticism from his fellow bishops but Patrick was convinced that he was doing the right thing by going 'to the furthest reaches of habitation, where no-one had previously ventured to baptise and ordain'.

Ordination of suitable candidates was a priority, 'so that there will be clergy everywhere to baptise and preach to a needy and receptive people'. In Christ, Patrick offered them hope, a sense of purpose and freedom from fear of pagan spells and curses. We can be sure that Patrick also healed the sick, for the early church practised healing with the same faith as the first apostles. Not surprisingly, there are many stories of Patrick healing the sick and raising the dead.

It is his ministry to the ordinary people of Ireland which is depicted opposite. Patrick raises his right hand to bless two old men, two young men and a young woman with a sleeping baby in her arms. We need not try to identify them: their Irish peasant faces are intended to be representative, for Patrick's mission was to *all* the Irish. God's approval is symbolised by Patrick's halo, which consists of doves flying from his head!

Michael Healy, 1908-9, Holy Trinity (C of I),
Magheralin, Co. Down

It was common for Christian missionaries to try to convert the rulers first, because the people were likely to follow their examples. That Patrick did so is clear from his many references to dealings with the Irish chiefs and their families. This is the context of one of the best known legends about Patrick, that of the Paschal fire: knowing that Loegaire was the most important of the Irish kings, Patrick goes towards his headquarters at Tara, County Meath. On Easter Even Patrick begins the traditional celebration of the festival by lighting the Paschal fire on the hill of Slane. Meanwhile, Loegaire and his court are celebrating a great pagan festival and there is a ban on any fire being lit before that at Tara. Loegaire is furious when he sees Patrick's fire and sends envoys to summon him to Tara.

It is this confrontation which Geddes shows. Behind Patrick, two of his followers clasp their hands nervously but they need not be afraid. The crudely drawn legs of the envoys show how primitive their ways are, while Patrick's indomitable figure indicates how the story will end. His huge feet remind us that he is going to proclaim the gospel of peace and Muirchú puts the words of a psalm on his lips: 'Some may go in chariots, and some on horses, but we will walk in the name of our God.'

Wilhelmina Geddes, 1923,
St Cedma's (C of I), Inver, Larne, Co. Antrim

Healy's cinquefoil panel is dominated by the flames of the Paschal fire, the effect of which is heightened by the gold flecks in Patrick's emerald robe. It looks as if the attending angels and the two kneeling figures below are shielding themselves from the blaze. The warrior, his spear at a useless angle, and the old man (possibly a druid), who in fright allows his scroll to fall on the ground, symbolise the futility of tribal warfare and pagan ways. In his left hand Patrick holds high the cross of salvation. It signifies his ministry among the Irish, whom he describes in his *Confession* as 'a people who, until now, always worshipped idols and impure things but have recently become the people of God and are now called the sons of God'.

At an early stage people came to believe that Patrick was more powerful than the wizards or druids. The legend of the Paschal fire reinforces this belief, for Loegaire relies on wizards but they are no match for Patrick. Loegaire gets so angry that he orders his men to kill Patrick, who cries: 'Let God arise and let his enemies be scattered.' Darkness falls at once, the earth shakes and, in confusion, the pagans turn on one another. Loegaire, pretending to be converted, still hopes to kill Patrick and his companions but they suddenly disappear and he sees a herd of deer in their place.

Michael Healy, 1914, Church of the Sacred Heart (RC),
Donnybrook, Co. Dublin

While Geddes uses the ancient Irish royal blue for the saint's robes, Clarke uses the nationalistic green, a notoriously hard colour for the stained glass artist. The same green appears in the shamrock in Patrick's hand. All over the world Irish people wear the shamrock on Saint Patrick's Day. The story that Patrick used the three leaflets of the shamrock to teach the doctrine of the Trinity is a modern addition to the legend but it points to a certain truth about Patrick. 'I must teach from the rule of faith in the Trinity,' he writes, and the creed which he includes in his *Confession* is a profession of faith in 'God the Father … and his son, Jesus Christ … and the Holy Spirit … whom we confess and adore as one God'.

Above Patrick's head an angel holds the cloth of heaven, in front of him stands the acolyte, Benignus. According to legend, Benignus was only a boy when Patrick baptised his father but he clung to the saint and begged to go along with him. Patrick was moved by his affection, baptised him, and gave him the name 'Benignus', meaning 'friendly'. Patrick realised that this youngster would eventually succeed him, so kept him close and nurtured him in the faith. Benignus is shown carrying a flaming torch, symbolising the light of the gospel which Patrick had brought.

Harry Clarke, 1915, Honan Chapel of St Finbarr,
University College Cork

The most significant aspect of this scene is the burst of sunlight behind the figures of Patrick and Elijah, as it represents 'Christ the true Sun, Jesus Christ, who will never die'. Patrick here adopts an image much used in the early church but he writes another complicated passage, in which he confuses the Greek word for sun (*Helios*) with the Latin name for Elijah (*Helias*). Thus he tells of a dream in which a huge rock fell on him and pinned him down. 'While I was crying "Elijah, Elijah!" with all my strength, the radiance of that sun fell on me and at once lifted all that burden from me and I believe that I was sustained by Christ my Lord.'

Patrick knew Christ as saviour and friend. Although it is now believed that the famous hymn *Saint Patrick's Breastplate* was not actually written by the saint, it does closely reflect his spirituality. A remarkable intimacy with Christ is revealed in the verse proclaiming His presence (trans. Kuno Meyer):

> Christ with me, Christ before me, Christ behind me,
> Christ in me, Christ beneath me, Christ above me,
> Christ on my right, Christ on my left,
> Christ when I lie down, Christ when I sit down,
> Christ when I arise.

*Michael Healy, 1908-9, Holy Trinity (C of I),
Magheralin, Co. Down*

Patrick's biblical teaching is highlighted in this (lower) section of the panel shown on page 40. Nessán, kneeling at Patrick's feet with a Bible in his hands, represents the generation of saints whom he taught and inspired. Many of these came to faith in their youth and were baptised and ordained by Patrick. They were the leaders of the church after Patrick's death and, although little is known about them, their tradition is carefully preserved. Nessán is remembered as the generous young man who provided food for the entertainers at a banquet in Patrick's honour. It was believed that Patrick founded a church for him at Mungret, County Limerick, in recognition of his generosity.

Patrick's theology is so thoroughly biblical and his writings so full of biblical phrases that he might be labelled a 'one-book-man'. He probably knew large sections of the Bible by heart and undoubtedly quoted liberally from it as he preached and taught. Among his many borrowings from St Paul is the reference to himself as 'a letter of Christ … written not with ink but with the Spirit of the living God'. This shows that Patrick saw not only the importance of the written gospel in carrying on the faith but also the vital role of the Holy Spirit in helping the Christian apply the gospel to the challenges of everyday life.

James Powell & Sons, 1910, St Mary's (C of I),
Howth, Co. Dublin

Patrick laid great emphasis on baptism and the eucharist as the two great sacraments ordained by Christ himself for the building up of believers. Among the 'many thousands' he baptised, he speaks of 'a very beautiful woman of noble birth'. After her baptism she wants to draw still closer to God and returns a few days later to ask his advice. She is convinced that God is calling her to be a nun and wins Patrick's wholehearted approval by doing so.

A similar but more dramatic story is depicted opposite. Although windows by the Clarke Studios are not nearly as exciting as those by Harry Clarke himself, this window well conveys the story of the baptism of the princesses. The seventh-century account of Patrick's missionary travels by Bishop Tirechán includes an encounter with Ethne and Fedelma, the daughters of Loegaire, at the well of Clébach in County Roscommon.

They ask Patrick questions about God and are so impressed by his answers that they are baptised at once. However, very eager to get close to God the princesses demand to see Christ's face. Patrick warns them that they cannot see Christ during this life, so they receive the eucharist and promptly die! Note how the end of the story is suggested by the tiny picture near the top of the window of Christ on the cross.

Clarke Studios, c. 1926, St Joseph's (RC), Carrickmacross,
Co. Monaghan

Given the context in which he wrote, it is not surprising that Patrick didn't talk about the eucharist. Yet the celebration of holy communion was the central act of the church's worship and was undoubtedly of the utmost importance to Patrick. This is what Hone seeks to convey here, with Patrick, Brigid and an angel presiding over a chalice.

All Patrick's hope was in Jesus Christ, 'who overcame death and was received back to God in heaven. God gave him all power over every name in heaven and earth and under the earth, that every tongue should confess that Jesus Christ is Lord and God … and we look for his coming again soon, as the judge of the living and the dead.' This biblical paraphrase in Patrick's creed points to an orthodox understanding of the eucharist as a commemoration of Christ's passion, a celebration of his resurrection and ascension, and a sign of hope for the future.

The bareness of Hone's setting suggests that Patrick was celebrating the eucharist in the open air. The magnificent, outsize chalice signifies the importance of the sacrament, not the splendour of the vessel which Patrick carried. On his travels Patrick probably took a simple communion set and improvised an altar when needed. Only at a later stage could a church be built as a focus for and witness to the spread of the faith.

Evie Hone, 1935, St Beaidh's (C of I),
Ardcarne, Co. Roscommon

Many windows deferentially show Patrick as a mitred bishop but O'Brien's portrayal of him as a shepherd is more accurate. Medieval rural society readily identified with the bishop as the shepherd of his people, modelled on Christ the Good Shepherd. Given his experience with sheep, it is not surprising that Patrick saw himself as the shepherd of his people. This is clear in his *Letter to the soldiers of Coroticus*, where he writes of his converts as 'sheep being mangled and carried off by robbers'. Then, deciding that the soldiers are worse than sheep rustlers, he continues: 'Savage wolves have devoured the Lord's flock,' and uses the imagery of a shepherd carefully building up a flock to convey the care with which he had increased the membership of the church. God's blessing on Patrick as pastor is suggested by the Heavenly Dove at the top and the Bible in his left hand.

Patrick does not mince his words but launches a blistering attack on the raiders. He calls them 'fellow-citizens of devils' and warns that they face torment and eternal death. Patrick had already sent a priest with a letter of protest and Coroticus's men had merely made fun of him. This time Patrick asks for a volunteer who will read the letter to Coroticus and his assembled people, in the hope that they will repent and find forgiveness.

Catherine O'Brien, 1939, St John's (C of I),
Malone, Belfast

NAOṁ
ṖAḊNAIƷ

Coroticus's raid was only one of countless times that Patrick confronted the power of evil. Irrespective of his success on that occasion, the legend that Patrick cast out all the snakes from Ireland refers to his victory over evil.

Healy's rendering takes artistic licence in turning the snake into a dragon. While a snake represents the stealthy, insinuating nature of evil, this fearsome dragon emphasises the danger of being over-powered, swallowed up by evil. Several men cower behind Patrick, relying on him to rescue them. The beast is nearly as big as he is but, like David against Goliath, he needs only a modest weapon – in his case a thin staff. It signifies Patrick's faith not in human power but in Christ's.

It was this faith that sustained Patrick in his internal struggle with evil. He talks openly about that struggle and knows how 'strong is the enemy who tries daily to turn me away from the faith'. Likewise, when betrayed by a close friend, he was tempted to give up and go home but, recognising that this would hand the victory to evil forces, he stood firm instead. Patrick believed that his fellow bishops were looking for an excuse to attack him and found it when an old friend reported a sin committed when Patrick was a boy. He was devastated by this rejection but was reassured by a dream in which he was called 'the apple of God's eye.' It is likely that one of his reasons for writing the *Confession* was to correct the record of his work in Ireland.

Michael Healy, 1908-9, Holy Trinity (C of I),
Magheralin, Co. Down

35

This is a good example of how a legend often conveys a truth. The panel shows Patrick impatiently waving away Seachnall, who is reciting the hymn he has composed in Patrick's honour. Patrick, who had been reluctant to allow Seachnall to write such a hymn, listens uneasily but cries 'Enough, Enough!' on hearing himself described as 'the greatest in the Kingdom of Heaven'. Wisely, he points out that such praise is reserved for God himself.

Seachnall, or Secundinus, was one of a group of fifth-century bishops working in the midlands. The Annals of Ulster say that they were sent to help Patrick but they may have come quite separately. The hymn to Patrick, *Audite omnes*, although attributed to Seachnall, is now known to be of a later date.

Patrick begins his *Confession* by styling himself 'a sinner and the least of all the faithful', and shows great awareness of his own weakness. 'I do not trust myself as long as I am in this earthly body,' he writes and, far from seeking praise, he attributes any success to God's transforming grace. Thus: 'It was not my own grace but God himself who overcame [all difficulties] in me ... I have been exalted beyond measure by the Lord and I did not deserve it.' In this respect the legend is perfectly accurate. For Patrick, it was reward enough to 'spend' himself in God's service.

Catherine O'Brien, 1914, Kilcurry (RC), Co. Louth

Patrick probably died peacefully in old age but that was not what he envisaged. 'I daily expect to be killed, ambushed or returned to slavery,' he wrote, 'but I fear none of these, for I have thrown myself into the hands of almighty God.' He even welcomed the prospect of martyrdom, saying: 'I ask God to grant that I may shed my blood in his name, even though I go without burial and my corpse be torn limb from limb by dogs or wild beasts, or the birds of the air devour it.'

If Patrick's burial place was recorded, the manuscript did not survive and ensuing generations had forgotten it but later legend placed his grave in Downpatrick, County Down.

The powerful figure drawn by Geddes, depicting the saint in old age, probably captures the historical Patrick better than any other window. An intensely deliberated picture of a complex character, it certainly does not fall into the all-too-frequent trap of portraying him as meek and mild! Patrick's strong head, his stern demeanour, the sinewy arm with which he grasps his staff, convey a rock-like intensity, reminiscent of St Peter and in complete harmony with the Patrick whom we see in his writings. The rich colouring of his clothes suggests the deep truths of the gospel he proclaims. The church is cradled so securely in his left hand that its future appears ensured.

Wilhelmina Geddes, 1923, St Cedma's (C of I),
Inver, Larne, Co. Antrim

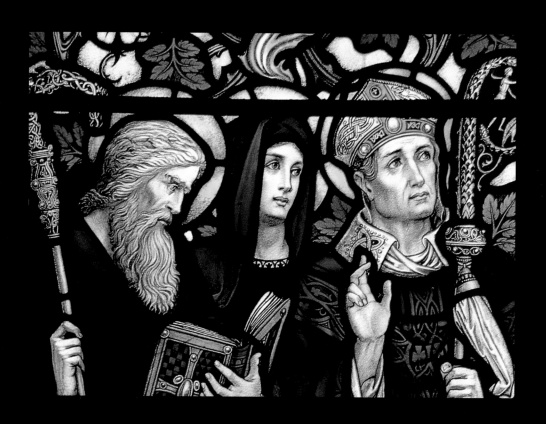

Here we have 'the three great Irish saints'. This is a section of a large window, in which all the figures are turned towards the risen Christ in acknowledgement of him as Lord. While Patrick and Brigid are looking at Christ, Columba, renowned for his scholarship, is engrossed in the Bible as if he is checking the Messianic prophesies. Patrick's clean-shaven face and fine features, perhaps intended to distinguish him from Columba, the Irishman, emphasise his sensitivity. Tough as he was, he often felt lonely and isolated. The drawing of Brigid suggests tenderness and patience, qualities not generally associated with Patrick or Columba.

Little is known about Brigid, except that she established an important foundation at Kildare. Many stories link her with Patrick but they are unreliable and probably arose from a later belief that all the early church leaders were Patrick's disciples.

Columba was certainly not Patrick's disciple, for he wasn't born until 521. Just as Patrick brought the gospel *from* Britain, Columba took it *to* Britain, when, in 563, he sailed to Scotland and established a monastery at Iona. From this centre Irish monks re-evangelised northern England, where the church had suffered during the Anglo-Saxon invasions. Thus an Irish spirituality restored the faith in Patrick's homeland.

James Powell & Sons, 1910, St Mary's (C of I),
Howth, Co. Dublin

This imposing *Te Deum Laudamus* window shows Christ in majesty, surrounded by a great array of saints, angels and cherubim. Patrick and Columba, are placed in the lower section, second from right, alongside Augustine of Canterbury, who was sent by the pope to reorganise the church in southern England in 597(the year of Columba's death), and Ambrose, the fourth-century writer and Bishop of Milan, suggesting equality of status. The saints join the apostles and angels in worshipping the risen Christ.

While the church in Europe and the Middle East had produced a sizeable body of literature before the fifth century, Patrick's writings constitute the earliest surviving Christian literature from Ireland or Britain. This makes them a vital historical source but, more than that, Patrick emerges as a compelling character, whose simple faith and absolute commitment remain a source of inspiration today.

Patrick is a central figure in the history of European Christianity and is celebrated worldwide as the apostle of Ireland. His feast day, celebrated on the continent since the ninth century, is equally celebrated in every country to which the Irish have subsequently emigrated.

Clayton & Bell, 1899, St Saviour's (C of I),
Arklow, Co. Wicklow

BIBLIOGRAPHY

de Paor, L., *St Patrick's World: The Christian Culture of Ireland's Apostolic Age: Translations and Commentaries*, Dublin,1993.

Duffy, J., *Patrick in his own Words*, (translation included), Dublin, 1985.

Hanson, R.P.C., *The Life and Writings of the historical Saint Patrick* (translation included), New York, 1983.

Hughes, K., *Church and Society in Ireland, A.D. 400-1200*, Collected studies edited by D. Dumville, London, 1987.

Whiteside, L., *The Spirituality of St Patrick*, Dublin, 1996.

The legends are comprehensively covered in:
de Breffny, B., *In the Steps of St Patrick*, London, 1982.
Healy, J., *The Life and Writings of St Patrick*, Dublin, 1905.

On nineteenth-century English stained glass:
Harrison, M., *Victorian Stained Glass*, London, 1980.
Larmour, P., *The Arts & Crafts Movement in Ireland,* Belfast, 1992.

For an introduction to twentieth-century Irish stained glass:
Bowe, N.G., Caron, D., and Wynne, M., *Gazetteer of Irish Stained Glass*, Dublin, 1988.

ACKNOWLEDGEMENTS

All unannotated quotations in this book come from St Patrick's writings, in my own translation. Complete translations are listed in the bibliography.

My thanks for advice and information on the stained glass primarily to Dr Paul Larmour; also to Dr David Lawrence, who introduced me to the appreciation of stained glass and has allowed us to use some of his slides, and to Dr David Caron and Dr Nicola Gordon Bowe. Thanks also to the Reverend Professor J.R Barlett for advice on aspects of the translation of Patrick's writings.